From Seed
to Pear

From Seed
to Pear

Ali Mitgutsch

 Carolrhoda Books, Inc., Minneapolis

First published in the United States of America 1981 by
Carolrhoda Books, Inc. All English language rights reserved.

Original edition © 1971 by Sellier Verlag GmbH, Eching bei München,
West Germany, under the title VOM KERN ZUR BIRNE.
Revised English text © 1981 by Carolrhoda Books, Inc.
Illustrations © 1971 by Sellier Verlag GmbH.

Manufactured in the United States of America

LIBRARY OF CONGRESS CATALOGING IN PUBLICATION DATA

Mitgutsch, Ali.
　From seed to pear.

　(A Carolrhoda start to finish book)
　A rev. English version of the author's Vom Kern zur
Birne, published in 1971.
　SUMMARY: Describes the cycle of a pear seed which,
when planted, produces a fruit-bearing tree and a supply
of new seeds.

　1. Pear—Juvenile literature. [1. Pear. 2. Seeds]
I. Title.

SB373.M5713　1981　　　　　634'.13　　　　　81-83
ISBN 0-87614-163-7

　　　　1　2　3　4　5　6　7　8　9　10　86　85　84　83　82　81

From Seed to Pear

Here is a pear that has been cut in half.

Inside the pear are seeds.

The gardener has dug a hole with his shovel.

He puts a pear seed into the hole.

Then he covers the seed with dirt.

The gardener waters the spot where he planted the seed.

Soon a small pear tree grows out of the ground.

The gardener ties the tree to a post
so that it will grow straight.

He also makes sure the tree gets plenty of water.

After many years the tree has grown big and strong.

In the spring it is covered with pretty blossoms.

One pear grows out of each blossom.

At first the pears are small and green and hard.

But as they grow, they become big and yellow and soft.

They are getting ripe.

When they are completely ripe,
the gardener picks the pears.
He puts them in a basket
and takes them to the market.

Many fruits and vegetables are sold at the market. This lady is selling tomatoes, plums, potatoes, bananas, and pears from our pear tree.

Ripe pears are sweet and juicy.
After a pear has been eaten,
only the stem and seeds will remain.
And then our story could begin all over again!

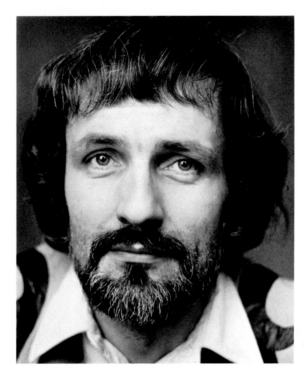

Ali
Mitgutsch

ALI MITGUTSCH is one of Germany's best-known children's book illustrators. He is a devoted world traveler, and many of his book ideas have taken shape during his travels. Perhaps this is why they have such international appeal. Mr. Mitgutsch's books have been published in 22 countries and are enjoyed by thousands of readers around the world.

Ali Mitgutsch lives with his wife and three children in Schwabing, the artists' quarter in Munich. The Mitgutsch family also enjoys spending time on their farm in the Bavarian countryside.

THE CAROLRHODA

 **START**

From Beet to Sugar

From Blossom to Honey

From Cacao Bean to Chocolate

From Cement to Bridge

From Clay to Bricks

From Cotton to Pants

From Cow to Shoe

From Dinosaurs to Fossils

From Egg to Bird

From Egg to Butterfly

From Fruit to Jam

From Grain to Bread

From Grass to Butter

From Ice to Rain

From Milk to Ice Cream

From Oil to Gasoline

From Ore to Spoon

From Sand to Glass

From Seed to Pear

From Sheep to Scarf

From Tree to Table

TO FINISH
BOOKS